COVER IMAGE

Roman woman from antiquity giving birth
to twins aided by midwives.

Parturition scene, Ostia, Italy (c. 400 BC–AD 300)
Attribution: CC0 1.0 Universal
Science Museum, London, UK

"This marble plaque depicts a 'parturition', or birthing scene. Such scenes eased the fears of expectant mothers by depicting positive birthing images. During this time, midwives were female. Men were not present at births unless a doctor was required in the case of a high status mother. Here, a woman reclines on a couch covered in drapes, attended by three women. They are dressed in classical Roman robes and one is holding the baby. The plaque was excavated at Ostia, Italy." – Science Museum category: Obstetrics, Gynaecology, and Contraception

"This publication offers an invaluable service to the church. It not only traces the history of ancient pagan and Christian views on abortion but also carefully explains how and why Christians throughout the centuries have advocated for universal human dignity."

DR. HANS BOERSMA
Professor of Ascetical Theology,
Nashotah House Theological Seminary

"This discourse offers a clear, coherent, and generous case for being holistically pro-life. *Being Human* shows the consistent value the Christian tradition has placed on human life, as well as the loss to our humanity that has happened since we have devalued infant life."

DR. MARIAM KOVALISHYN
Associate Professor, New Testament and
Classical Literature, Regent College

"A wonderfully-argued and referenced presentation of the continuous Christian witness for life, from the earliest centuries until fifteen minutes ago."

DR. FREDERICA MATHEWES-GREEN
Artist, Author, and Podcaster for
Ancient Faith Radio (Orthodox)

"Written from thirty-five years' experience of helping women and children in crisis, *Being Human* is a must-read for anyone seeking to understand the issue of abortion from a sound theological and pastoral perspective."

MOST REV. J. MICHAEL MILLER, CSB
Archbishop, Roman Catholic Archdiocese of Vancouver

ADDITIONAL ENDORSERS

VERY REV. JOHN BRECK
Orthodox Theologian and Ethicist

DR. MARGARET COTTLE
Palliative Care Physician, Clinical Assistant Professor

REV. MARDI DOLFO-SMITH
Executive Pastor, Alliance Canada

DR. NATASHA FERNANDES
Psychiatrist, Clinical Assistant Professor

FAYTENE GRASSESCHI
Producer and TV Show Host

DR. MARGARET HARTSHORN
Board Chair, Heartbeat International

REV. ELIZABETH JØRGENSEN
Lead Pastor, Foursquare Church of Canada

DR. LAURA LEWIS
Executive Director, Pregnancy Care Canada

REV. WENDY LOWE
Executive Director, Defend Dignity

ANDREA MROZEK
Senior Fellow, Cardus Institute

DR. KIM PHÚC PHAN THỊ
Founder, KIM Foundation International

MAT. VALERIE PROTOPAPAS
Co-founder, Orthodox Christians for Life

DR. JOAN SCHULTZ
Psychologist, Postsecondary Educator

DR. MARGARET SOMERVILLE
Bioethicist and Legal Scholar

DR. SARAH WILLIAMS
Research Professor, Christian History

DR. DAVID T. WOOD
Senior Associate Pastor, Adjunct Professor

DR. GLORIA WOODLAND
Director, Chaplaincy Program, MB Seminary

BEING HUMAN

BEING HUMAN

ABORTION AND THE CHURCH

BRIAN NORTON

BEING HUMAN

Abortion and the Church

BRIAN NORTON

Book design and production
PearCreative.ca

ISBN: 978-1-0689334-0-0 (Print)

To eight remarkable women and girls—my co-conspirator in life, Judi; our daughters, Laura, Carly, and Alexandra; and grand-punks Chloe, Brooklynn, Maddison, and Josephine.

I am blessed beyond measure.

ACKNOWLEDGEMENTS

I am indebted to two brilliant friends, Ginimi Chan and Sara Chang, who graciously persevered in the editing process over content, context, and syntax. Thank you, Ginimi. Thank you, Sara.

Therapy has helped.

CONTENTS

PROLOGUE

DISCLAIMERS

For some forty years by vocation and volunteering, I have been focused on the provision of support services for women and children at risk. So, to pen a paper solely about the ethics of abortion is normally not my go-to métier.

I am sensitive that some readers may have had an abortion or have suggested an abortion to others. Please do not take anything I say as judgmental. Our Lord is forgiving and he abounds in compassion. Further, I am sensitive to the blunt words about abortion used by our Church Fathers, ecclesiastical leaders, theologians, and first-wave feminists. The language is strong.

My intention throughout this discourse is not to necessarily convey progressive or conservative values, but biblical values. Forgive me where I miss the mark.

As followers of Jesus—whether Catholic, Orthodox, or Protestant—our beliefs, values, and conduct are tethered to Scripture. Without God, and without his communicated principles and morals, we fall into a rabbit hole of ethical relativism. Without God, as atheist Jean-Paul Sartre famously lectured:

> *There can no longer be any good a priori, since there is no infinite and perfect consciousness to think it. It is nowhere written that 'the good' exists, that one must be honest or must not lie, since we are now upon the plane where there are only men. Dostoevsky once wrote: 'If God did not exist, everything would be permitted;' and that, for existentialism, is the starting point. Everything is indeed permitted if God does not exist, and man is in consequence forlorn, for he cannot find anything to depend upon either within or outside himself.*[1]

---

1) "Existentialism Is a Humanism," in *Jean-Paul Sartre: Basic Writings*, trans. Stephen Priest (London: Routledge, 2001), 32.

EASIER TO LABEL

On this highly-charged human rights debate, it can be easier to label one's "opponent" than to choose to respectfully hear and understand her or his perspective. The epithets "pro-life" and "pro-choice" (or "anti-abortion" and "pro-abortion") obviously oversimplify what an individual may actually think and feel about abortion. For example, for persons identifying as pro-life, their detractors (often without warrant) can misconstrue *them* as simply being "single-issue" adherents. For persons who identify as pro-choice, this does not necessarily mean they are advocates for abortion on demand or for late-term abortion.

Cognizant of the above, for a pro-life definition I will use this brief explanation which adequately captures a congruent understanding for the respect for all members of the human family:

> *Life is a gift from God for us to respect and protect through all its stages, from conception to natural death. Every person is created by God, in his image, and loved by him. Each person's*

> *life has inherent worth and dignity. This belief compels…[us] to support the protection and promotion of life, to oppose practices that destroy or devalue human life, and to uphold the dignity of every person.*[2]

2) "Sanctity of Life," abridged, Evangelical Fellowship of Canada, accessed May 5, 2024, www.evangelical fellowship.ca/Themes/Sanctity-of-Life.

INTRODUCTION

A dear friend forwarded a blog post on the subject of abortion penned by a thoughtful, theologically liberal pastor. My friend asked for my opinion. I got carried away—thus, this booklet, *Being Human: Abortion and the Church.*

The blog writer was sincere and conciliatory in his provocative piece but, alas, his two major conclusions on abortion (quoted here below) are mistaken:[3]

1. "Christian thinking on the issue has not always been what it is now."

3) I have other points of disagreement with the author's blog post, but they are small potatoes.

2. "There are good reasons to land on either side of this issue from Christian conviction."

First, people may disagree with Judeo-Christian ethics on abortion. But Christian thinking, historically and theologically, is unabashedly pro-life. This is not to say there are not exceptions about the ethics of abortion by various theologically liberal or progressive individuals. In fact, there are a number of mainline Protestant denominations which are permissive about abortion, including the United Church of Canada, the United Church of Christ, and the Episcopal Church (USA).

Second, the "good reasons" land decisively on not supporting abortion as a Christian conviction.

What follows is an examination of the views and practices of the universal Christian Church—Catholic, Orthodox, and Protestant—both epoch and present day, on the morality of abortion and our pastoral call for helping women experiencing unexpected pregnancies.

CHAPTER ONE

ABORTION IN THE ANCIENT WORLD

FROM ANTIQUITY

The devaluing of children in the womb is not unique to our own generation. Abortion and infanticide were freely practised in pagan societies before and during the time of Christ. Pagan writers attest to the universality of abortion. As historiographer Michael J. Gorman documents, "Rich and poor, slave and free, young and old aborted themselves and were given abortions."[4]

Plato and Aristotle both supported abortion on demand. Further, Plato held that any pregnant woman over 40 years of age must abort.[5] Aristotle argued that handicapped infants should be left to die of exposure (a sharp contrast to our Lord's call to love people with infirmities as persons of worth).[6]

The Greeks procured abortion by means of medicinal abortifacients. The Persians terminated pregnancies using surgical tools inside the birth canal. The ancient Hindus and Arabs subjected women to vaginally inserted chemical abortifacients.[7]

---

4) Michael J. Gorman, *Abortion and the Early Church: Christian, Jewish, and Pagan Attitudes in the Greco-Roman World* (Eugene: Wipf and Stock Publishers, 1982), 27.

5) Paul B. Fowler, *Abortion: Toward an Evangelical Consensus* (Portland: Multnomah Press, 1987), 16. See Plato, *The Republic*, Book V, 460 b-c and 460e-461c.

6) Fowler, *Abortion*, 16. See Aristotle, *Historia Animalium* 7.3; and Aristotle, *Politics* 7.1.1, 7.14.10.

7) George Devereux, "A Typological Study of Abortion in 350 Primitive, Ancient, and Pre-Industrial Societies," in Harold Rosen, ed., *Abortion in America* (Boston: Beacon Press, 1967), quoted in George Grant, *Grand Illusions: The Legacy of Planned Parenthood*, 2nd ed., (Franklin: Adroit Press, 1992), 209. See also Gorman, *Abortion and the Early Church*, 15-18.

The waists of Chinese mothers were bound so tightly they would abort. In Japan, pregnant women straddled boiling cauldrons of parricidal mixtures. The stomachs of pregnant Polynesians were beaten with stones.[8] In Egypt, newborns were harvested for ingredients used in the manufacturing of cosmetic creams.[9]

In addition, unwanted babies in the Greco-Roman world were commonly left outside the city walls to die from exposure and by predatory birds, animals, and stray dogs. Infanticide was so "natural" that playwrights would make fun of the practice in comedies.[10] Female gendercide was the most frequent. Girls were discarded alive in garbage dumps.[11] Sewers

---

8) George Grant, *Third Time Around: A History of the Pro-Life Movement from the First Century to the Present* (Brentwood, TN: Wolgemuth and Hyatt, 1991), 12.

9) Grant, *Illusions*, 209. Grant cites for further reading, Augustus Ambrose, *The Women of Gilead: The Abuse of Women and Children in History* (New York: Uptown Bookseller, 1957).

10) Ken Spiro, *World Perfect: The Jewish Impact on Civilization* (Deerfield Beach: Simcha Press, 2002), 18.

11) Mike Aquilina, *The Witness of Early Christian Women: Mothers of the Church* (Huntington: Our Sunday Visitor Publishing, 2014), 15.

would clog with female newborns.[12] In referring to daughters, a common adjective was "odious".[13]

Papyrus Oxyrhynchus 120 contains a letter from a husband, Hilarion, to his pregnant wife, Alis:

> *Know that I am still in Alexandria. And do not worry if they all come back and I remain in Alexandria. I ask and beg you to take good care of our baby son, and as soon as I receive payment I shall send it up to you. If you are delivered of a child [before I get home], if it is a boy keep it, if a girl discard it.*[14]

Needless to say, the ancient Greeks and Romans were not alone in their inhumanity to those who were weak, vulnerable, or deemed worthless. "The Asian civilizations, just like the European ones, were largely devoid of the values we hold precious. They had human sacrifice, infanticide, and caste systems," chronicles antiquities historian, Rabbi Ken Spiro. "Yes, they had beautiful philosophies, but we must make a distinction

---

12) Rodney Stark, *The Rise of Christianity* (New York: HarperOne, 1996), 118, referenced in David Wood, "Early Church Expansion, Life and Worship" (course, Pacific Life Bible College, Surrey, BC, 2022), Lecture 2.

13) Aquilina, *Early Christian Women*, 15.

14) Spiro, *Jewish Impact*, 16.

between cultural and technological sophistication and the moral and ethical reality of a society."[15]

CRAFTED IN GOD'S IMAGE

In contrast, our Judeo-Christian God affirms the sanctity of human life. Foundational to this view of humankind is the *imago Dei*. Genesis Chapter One lays down a worldview upon which the rest of the Law and the Scriptures are based:

> *So God created mankind in his own image, in the image of God he created them; male and female he created them. (Genesis 1:27)*

Michelangelo, Creación de Adán, Sistine Chapel Ceiling (AD 1511), Rome, fresco, CC0.

---

15) Spiro, *Jewish Impact*, 72.

From all Biblical accounts, human life is sacred—*sui generis*, unique. All human life has intrinsic value, not because of developmental milestones or a societal validation of worth, but because we are created in God's image.[16]

Jesus has entrusted to his people the responsibility to advocate, prophetically and pastorally, on behalf of all among us who are devalued—those impoverished, afflicted, oppressed, displaced, widowed, or orphaned—whoever may be cast as *the least of these*.

From the Matthew 25 passage, two important traditions would develop in the universal Church. In the Protestant tradition, followers of Jesus Christ are an extension of his compassionate care for those in need or devalued. In the Catholic and Orthodox tradition, by serving the afflicted we are, in fact, serving the "hidden Christ".

---

16) In the words of Orthodox ethicist John Breck, "Personhood is conferred by God and not by physiological development, medical analysis, or social convention. *Know that the Lord himself is God; It is he who has made us, and not we ourselves.*" John Breck, *The Sacred Gift of Life: Orthodox Christianity and Bioethics* (Crestwood, NY: St. Vladimir's Seminary Press, 1998), 149. To read more on the imago Dei, see Edwin Hui, "Personhood and Bioethics," and Bruce Waltke, "Love, Justice and the Allocation of Limited Medical Resources," in *Questions of Right and Wrong: The Proceedings of the 1993 Clinical Bioethics Conference*, ed. Edwin C. Hui (Vancouver: Regent College, 1994), 1-15, 75-91.

As we will observe, the grace of the Gospel, and the conduct of the Church, would elevate the worth and dignity of women, and would curb widespread abortion and infanticide throughout much of the Western world.

CHAPTER TWO

CHURCH OPPOSITION TO ABORTION

FLEDGLING CHURCH

I will now cover two millenniums of church history. 😐

As we have seen, abortion in antiquity—with the exception of the Jews—was frequent and widespread.[17] It would not be until the birth of the Church that

---

17) "[A]bortion, like exposure, was unacceptable [among the Jews], and this was well-known in the ancient world." Gorman, *Abortion and the Early Church*, 33. Consider reading Rabbi Ken Spiro's book, *World Perfect: The Jewish Impact on Civilization.*

there was to be substantial opposition to abortion, infanticide, and abandonment. The Gospel changed people's hearts to a higher view of human life.

Women and children were perceived as subhuman in the prevailing Greco-Roman world. Radically, Jesus and his apostles affirmed the humanity and dignity of everyone—irrespective of gender, age, economic status, social position, or ethnicity.

Christian converts were disproportionally women. Women welcomed the Christian ban of abortion, infanticide, and gender selection.[18] Women welcomed the Christian prohibition of incest, marital infidelity, and polygamy. Pagan men prized female chastity. For Christians, premarital chastity was to be mutual for both men and women.[19]

Females were given higher status in the fledgling, egalitarian Christian community than in the surrounding pagan world. Christianity would

---

18) David Wood, "Early Church Expansion, Life and Worship," Lecture 2. Wood cites the following: Rodney Stark, *The Rise of Christianity*, chpt 5; Larry Hurtado, *Destroyer of the gods* (Waco: Baylor University Press, 2016); Alan Kreider, *The Patient Ferment of the Early Church* (Grand Rapids: Baker Academic, 2016), chpt 5; Sarah Williams, "History of Christianity I" (course, Regent College, Vancouver, BC, 2017), Lecture 3.

19) Hurtado, *Destroyer of the gods*, 157, 166-167.

scandalize Roman family values. Women and children were treated as persons. Pagan philosopher Celsus would bemoan the new lived reality of Christian men conversing with "slaves, stupid women, little children, and fools."[20]

Gender parity at the offering table. Third century fresco, Callistus Catacomb, Rome. Wilpert, *Malereien*, pl. 41.1, CC0.

20) Alexander Roberts and James Donaldson, eds., *The Ante-Nicene Fathers: Translations of the Writings of the Fathers Down to AD 325* (New York: Charles Scribner's Sons, 1903), quoted in Mike Aquilina, *The Witness of Early Christian Women: Mothers of the Church* (Huntington: Our Sunday Visitor Publishing, 2014), 22.

Woman raising the Cup. Marcellino and Pietro Catacomb, Rome, c. late AD 200s. Wilpert, *Malereien*, pl. 157.2, CC0.

In Corinth, Christians provided residential care for prostitutes experiencing crisis pregnancies. In Rome, Christians would rescue babies left to die of exposure and bring them home to raise as their own.[21] Patristics scholar Mike Aquilina explains, "In the early days, when there were more slave traders than Christians, a girl—for that matter, a boy—rescued from the rubbish heap was most likely to end up in a brothel. These were brothels that specialized in young children."[22]

21) Grant, *Illusions*, 214.

22) Aquilina, *Early Christian Women*, 16.

PRESERVED DOCUMENTS

In stark contrast to all the prevailing cultures, first and second century documents show that abortion was never acceptable in the Church.

The *Didache*—anonym, *The Teachings of the Twelve Apostles*—was a codification of the oral tradition of the Apostles read universally among the early churches, which included: "You shall not procure an abortion, nor destroy a newborn child."[23] From the theologian, Clement of Alexandria, in the *Paedagogus* (c. AD 96) on abortifacients: "For those … taking stimulating drugs to bring on an abortion wholly lose their own humanity along with the fetus."[24]

From the *Letter of Barnabas* (c. AD 70): "You shall not slay the child by abortion. You shall not kill that which has already been generated."[25] This in the early apologetic *Letter of Mathetes to Diognetus* (c. AD 130) contrasting the life of Christians with that of non-Christians: "They marry, as do all others;

23) *The Didache, 2*, 1-2; cf. *II Thessalonians* 2:15.

24) Clement of Alexandria, *Paedagogus*, Book III.

25) *Letter of Barnabas* 19.5; preserved in the 4th century *Codex Sinaiticus*.

they beget children, but they do not destroy their offspring."[26]

From Tertullian, the acknowledged founder of Western theology, in the *Apology* (AD 197): "To hinder a birth is merely a speedier way to kill a human. It does not matter if you take away a life that has been born, or destroy one that is not yet born."[27]

THE INCARNATION

Ghirlandaio, The Visitation (AD 1491), tempera on panel.
Louvre Museum, Paris, Sailko, CC0.

26) *Letter of Mathetes to Diognetus*, Chapter 5: "The Manners of the Christians."

27) Tertullian, *Apology*, 9.8.

Our redemptive Christian faith began in the womb. "But the angel said to her, 'Do not be afraid, Mary; you have found favour with God. You will conceive and give birth to a son, and you are to call him Jesus'" (Luke 1:30-31). The early Church understood that Jesus did not become a human on the day of his birth, but nine months earlier at the Incarnation, at the *Conceptio Christ.*[28]

Further from Scripture,[29] the Visitation also bears witness to the humanity of the fetus.

> *When Elizabeth heard Mary's greeting, the baby leaped in her womb, and Elizabeth was filled with the Holy Spirit. In a loud voice she exclaimed: "Blessed are you among women, and blessed is the child you will bear! But why am I so favoured, that the mother of my Lord should come to me? As soon as the sound of*

---

28) Frederica Mathewes-Green, "The Pro-Life Cause, Orthodoxy, and Hope," Ancient Faith Ministries, January 12, 2012, https://blogs.ancientfaith.com/blogs/. Consider reading *De Anima* by Tertullian, followed by the *Evangelium Vitae* by John Paul II.

29) Other examples from Scripture pertaining to the imago Dei and God's divine interaction regarding conception and fetuses: Genesis 1:26-27; Psalm 8:3-8; Genesis 29:31; Genesis 30:22; Judges 13:3-5; Ruth 4:13; Luke 1:15; Job 10:8-12; Psalm 127:3; Psalm 139:13-16; Ecclesiastes 11:5; Isaiah 49:1,5; Jeremiah 1:5; Luke 1:15; Luke 1:39-44; and Galatians 1:15.

your greeting reached my ears, the baby in my womb leaped for joy." (Luke 1:41-44)

THE CANONS

Not only was the early Church and the earliest theologians united against abortion, but so were the other Church Fathers and apologists throughout the generations: Athenagoras, Hippolytus, Felix, Origen, Cyprian, Gregory, Basil, Ambrose, Jerome, Chrysostom, Augustine, Photius, and others.[30] On the moral issue of abortion there was never a dissenting opinion by a Church Father or in patristic tradition.[31]

---

30) Athenagoras (c. AD 133–190), *A Plea Regarding Christians*, chap. 35. Hippolytus (c. AD 170–235), *Refutation of All Heresies*, Book 9, chap. 7. Minucius Felix (n.d.–c. AD 250), *Octavius*, chap. 30. Origen (c. AD 185–253), *Contra Celsum*, 3.61-62. Cyprian (c. AD 210–258), *Novatus*, Epistle 48, chap. 2. Basil (c. AD 330–379), *Canonica Prima*, 188.2. Gregory (AD 335–394), "On the Soul and the Resurrection," *The Sacred Writings of Gregory of Nyssa*. Ambrose (c. AD 339–397), *Hexameron*, chap. 18. Chrysostom, *Homilies on Romans*, 24, 3.4.1. Jerome (c. AD 347–420), *Letter to Eustochium*, XXII, point 13. Augustine (AD 354–430), *On Marriage and Concupiscence* (Book I), chap. 17. Photius (c. AD 810–893), *Photian Collection* (Christian teachings on abortion catalogued).

31) Alexander Webster, "An Orthodox Word on Abortion" (Paper delivered at the Consultation on The Church and Abortion, Princeton, 1992), 8-9. See also the Holy Orthodox Church, "An Orthodox View of Abortion," *Brief Amicus Curiae of the Holy Orthodox Church*, No. 88-605, submitted to the Supreme Court of the United States, February 21, 1989, accessed July 5, 2023, http://orthodoxkansas.org/Orthodox_Amicus_Curiae_brief.html.

Later, the canonical prohibition of abortion would be pronounced by the Synod of Elvira (c. AD 303), followed by the Synod of Ancyra (AD 314), and followed by the Quinisext Ecumenical Council (AD 691). The Ecumenical Patriarch of Constantinople would catalogue the Christian teachings on abortion into the *Photian Collection*, and these canons were subsequently ratified by the Church (AD 883).[32]

Following Constantine and the "Christianization" of the Roman Empire, laws prohibiting abortion were established. Abortion was denounced throughout the Byzantine millennium (AD 330 to 1453). Moral opposition to abortion continued following the East-West Schism, the Reformation (including Thomas Aquinas, Martin Luther, and John Calvin), and beyond.[33]

---

32) Holy Orthodox Church, *Brief Amicus Curiae*; Breck, *Orthodox Christianity and Bioethics*, 152; and Matushka Valerie H. Protopapas, "The Position of the Church on Abortion," Pemptousia (website), St. Maxim the Greek Institute, April 20, 2016, https://pemptousia.com/2016/04/the-position-of-the-church-on-abortion-2/.

33) Thomas Aquinas (c. 1225–1274), *Summa Theologica*. Martin Luther (1483–1546), *What Luther Says: An Anthology*, comp. Ewald M. Plass, vol. 2, no. 2826, (St. Louis: Concordia, 1959), 905. John Calvin (1509–1564), *Commentaries on the Four Last Books of Moses* (Grand Rapids: Eerdmans, 1950), 41-42.

It is important to address a misconception by some that Aquinas' view about delayed hominization, or ensoulment, opens the door for abortion. *Summa Theologica* offers no defense of abortion at any gestational stage.[34] "In the 13th century, St. Thomas Aquinas made extensive use of Aristotle's thought, including his theory that the rational human soul is not present in the first few weeks of pregnancy." Nevertheless, as the US Conference of Catholic Bishops further explains, "But [Aquinas] also rejected abortion as gravely wrong at every stage, observing that it is a sin 'against nature' to reject God's gift of a new life."[35]

---

34) Embryo Project Encyclopedia, s.v. "St. Thomas Aquinas (c. 1225–1274)," by Katherine Brind'Amour, published November 11, 2007, accessed May 13, 2023, https://embryo.asu.edu/pages/st-thomas-aquinas-c-1225-1274: "*Summa Theologica* offers no defense of abortion as a permissible act at any stage in the pregnancy, but it does specify that once the fetus has become animated (when he believed ensoulment of the living human being took place), it is homicide to kill it. This measure of ensoulment or delayed hominization … is typically equated with the stage at which quickening took place—defined by Aristotle as forty days for boys and eighty days after conception for girls."

35) "Respect for Unborn Human Life: The Church's Constant Teaching," United States Conference of Catholic Bishops, accessed March 11, 2023, https://www.usccb.org/issues-and-action/human-life-and-dignity/abortion/respect-for-unborn-human-life.

RECENT PAST

During the twentieth century, prominent ecclesiastical leaders continued to publicly affirm the intrinsic value of preborn children at all gestational stages. This included Protestant theologians Dietrich Bonhoeffer, Karl Barth, and Helmut Thielicke.[36, 37]

This includes all Orthodox patriarchs. Codified in its official Ecclesiastical Law Book, the Eastern Orthodox

---

36) Dietrich Bonhoeffer, *Ethics*, trans. N.H. Smith (New York: Macmillan, 1955), chap. 3; Karl Barth, "Reproduction and the Nascent of Life," *Church Dogmatics*, trans. G.W. Bromiley and T.E. Torrance, vol. 3 (Edinburgh: T. & T. Clark, 1961), pt. 4; and Helmut Thielicke, "Interruption of Pregnancy: The Problem of Artificial Abortion," *The Ethics of Sex* (New York: Harper and Row, 1964), chap. B, 226-247.

37) Some students of Barth have wondered if he allowed for a possibility of abortion in a rare circumstance (beyond saving the life of the mother). For example, one law professor characterizes Barth's position as being "anti-choice," though not necessarily definitively "pro-life." See Michael W. McConnell, "Religion and the Search for a Principled Middle Ground on Abortion," *Michigan Law Review* 92(6), (1994): 1905, https://repository.law.umich.edu/mlr/vol92/iss6/36/. McConnell is discussing Elizabeth Mensch and Alan Freeman, *The Politics of Virtue: Is Abortion Debatable*? (Durham: Duke University Press, 1993), who are discussing Barth, Bonhoeffer, and others. This is too nuanced for an adequate deliberation here. But what is certain: First, Barth believed abortion to be a "monstrous" killing of a child (*Dogmatics*, 415-417). Second, there is "divine mercy" for the repentant: "[If]… abortion is irrefutably seen to be sin, murder, and transgression, it cannot possibly be maintained that there is no forgiveness for this sin" (*Dogmatics*, 419). Amen. Amen.

Church from its inception has not, and will not, alter its moral position on abortion.[38]

This also includes all Catholic popes. Promulgated in the *Catechism of the Catholic Church*, preborn children have a God-ordained inviolable right to life: "Since the first century the Church has affirmed the moral evil of every procured abortion. This teaching has not changed and remains unchangeable (*n* 2271)."[39]

38) John Kowalczyk, *An Orthodox View of Abortion* (Minneapolis: Gopher State Litho, 1977), 15.

39) Libreria Editrice Vaticana, *Catechism of the Catholic Church* (Washington, DC: United States Conference of Catholic Bishops, 2008).

CHAPTER THREE

THE CHANGE OF TIDE

FEMINISM

Feminist foremothers were pro-life. These egalitarian activists fought for women's suffrage, proprietorship, for legal guardianship of children, temperance, labour reforms, advocated pacifism, and were resolutely anti-abortion and anti-eugenics.

Feminist Serrin M. Foster, creator of the Women Deserve Better® campaign, writes: "Without known exception, our feminist foremothers opposed abortion, and—like Susan B. Anthony—sought to address the root causes that drive women to abortion."[40] The first-wave feminist leadership frequently referred to abortion as "ante-natal murder" and "ante-natal infanticide."[41]

Elizabeth Cady Stanton, Susan B. Anthony, and Alice Paul were three of the foremost early feminists, suffragists, equal rights activists, and pro-life advocates of the twentieth century women's movement. Stanton and Anthony would voice their opposition to abortion in their feminist newspaper publication, *The Revolution*. The practice was unanimously reviled in more than one hundred editorials and articles.[42]

---

40) Serrin M. Foster, "Feminist Foremothers," Feminists for Life of America, accessed May 15, 2023, https://www.feministsforlife.org/herstory. Foster served on the US National Taskforce Against Sexual Assault and Domestic Violence. Foster is president of Feminists for Life.

41) Mary K. Derr, Rachel MacNair, and Linda Naranjo-Huebl, *Prolife Feminism: Yesterday and Today* (Kansas City: Feminism and Nonviolence Studies Association, 2005), quoted in Cat Clark, "The Truth About Susan B. Anthony," Feminists for Life of America, accessed May 15, 2023, https://www.feministsforlife.org/the-truth-about-susan-banthony/.

42) Colleen Kelly Spellecy and Eric Anthony,"Yes, Susan B. Anthony Was Pro-Life: She and Elizabeth Cady Stanton railed against abortion in the pages of their paper," *The Wall Street Journal*, June 13, 2022.

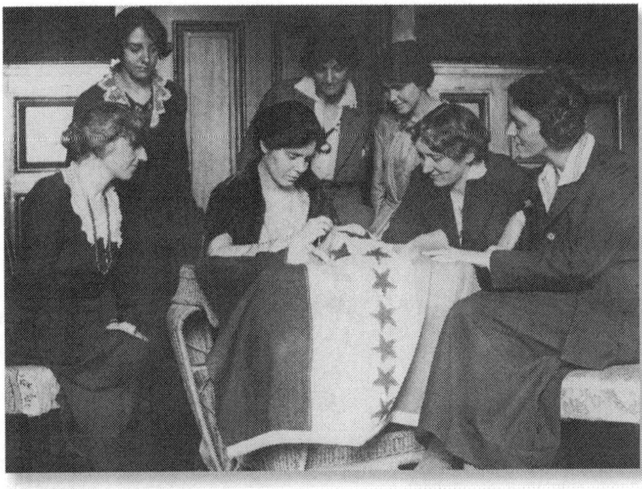

Alice Paul (sitting, ctr-left) with other feminist activists sewing stars on a suffragist flag. Library of Congress, CC0.

Alice Paul tirelessly organized marches, led hunger strikes, was beaten multiple times, and arrested repeatedly during her non-violent campaigns for equality for women. In 1920, Paul would become co-author of the original *19th Amendment to the U.S. Constitution: Women's Right to Vote.* In 1954, she was instrumental in establishing a permanent United Nations Commission on the Status of Women. On the worth and dignity of preborn children: "How can one protect and help women by killing them as babies," Paul would adamantly declare. "Abortion is the ultimate in the exploitation of women."[43]

Beginning in the early 1960s, the second-wave feminist movement fought against systemic patriarchy and advanced policies for societal/political equality, ending violence against women, legalized birth control and, in contrast to their Christian feminist peers, uncompromisingly pivoted to advocating for legal abortion access.[44] Today, there remains a deep ethical divide between Christian feminists, who are

---

43) Serrin M. Foster, "Women Deserve Better Than Abortion: The Ultimate Exploitation of Women," *National Review*, January 19, 2018, https://www.nationalreview.com/2018/01/womens-march-pro-life-feminists/.

44) The second-wave feminist fight for abortion had a checkered evolution. Friends and foes of Planned Parenthood founder, Margaret Sanger, question some of her motives and practices. The current CEO of Planned Parenthood says, "Margaret Sanger harmed a generation with her beliefs." From Alexis McGill Johnson, "I'm the Head of Planned Parenthood. We're Done Making Excuses for Our Founder: We must reckon with Margaret Sanger's association with white supremacist groups and eugenics," *New York Times*, April 17, 2021, https://www.nytimes.com/2021/04/17/opinion/planned-parenthood-margaret-sanger.html. Margaret Sanger aside, for profiles on renowned feminists, visit the Feminists for Life webpage, "Feminist Foremothers," accessed May 15, 2023, http://www.feministsforlife.org/herstory/. For an overview of the feminist movement in Canada, visit *Canadian Encyclopedia,* "Early Women's Movements in Canada: 1867-1960," published August 15, 2016, https://www.thecanadianencyclopedia.ca/en/article/early-womens-movements-incanada and "Women's Movements in Canada: 1960-85," published September 12, 2016, https://www.thecanadianencyclopedia.ca/en/ article/womens-movements-in-canada-196085.

fundamentally pro-life, and agnostic or atheistic feminists who are fundamentally pro-choice.

A crucial question: can one authentically be feminist and pro-life? Christian feminists say, yes. Regarding the wider population, in a Canadian poll, 57% of the female respondents said, yes.[45] However, as author Andrea Mrozek remarks, "The bigger question is whether the second-wave can embrace the first wave—their own history. When they do, the feminist world will get a lot more reasonable, inclusive, and a whole lot larger."[46]

PRO-WOMEN

As we have seen, the *philia* and *agape* action of the Church essentially curbed abortion and infanticide up to our own era, more or less to the early 1960s. During the late twentieth century, a humanistic worldview and situational ethics eroded the Judeo-Christian base for moral absolutes. Out went the sacredness (the intrinsic value) of human life. Today, preborn infants,

---

45) Andrea Mrozek, "Celebrating Women," *Cardus*, last modified March 8, 2017, https://www.cardus.ca/news/news-releases/celebrating-women/.

46) Andrea Mrozek, "Women's Happiness, Women's Health: The Feminist Fight Against Abortion," *Cardus*, last modified March 4, 2019, https://www.cardus.ca/research/family/research-report/womens-happiness-womens-health/.

babies born with infirmities, people frail and aged, are again seen as expendable and disposable. Grievously, the devaluation of females is also a recurring reality with our postmodern world.

Mother Teresa taught that abortion undeniably is anti-female: "Three-quarters of its victims are women: Half the babies and all the mothers."[47] The Nobel Peace Prize recipient famously explained:

> *The so-called right to abortion has pitted mothers against their children and women against men. It has sown violence and discord at the heart of the most intimate human relationships. It has aggravated the derogation of the father's role in an increasingly fatherless society. It has portrayed the greatest of gifts—a child—as a competitor, an intrusion, and an inconvenience.*[48]

The diminishing and erasing of girls is unabated. As in the pre-Judeo-Christian world, female fetuses

---

47 Churches of St. Paul and St. Michael, "Pro-Life Quotes," Worship, accessed August 2, 2023, https://www.stpaulstmichael.com/copy-of-prayers-reflections.

48) Mother Teresa, "Mother Teresa's 1994 Message to the Supreme Court on Abortion," *Public Discourse: The Journal of the Witherspoon Institute*, September 5, 2016, https://www.thepublicdiscourse.com/2016/09/17771/.

are particularly targeted. Today, there are between 80 million to 100 million "missing girls" from sex-selective abortion and infanticide. All discarded for simply being female.[49] In Canada, abortion-induced gendercide is permitted and takes place.[50]

God bless our contemporary, countercultural, pro-women, pro-life advocates. Such undaunted, multifarious women include Dr. Margaret Cottle, Serrin M. Foster, Faytene Grasseschi, Dr. Margaret Hartshorn, Patricia Heaton, Abby Johnson, Rev. Alveda King, Dr. Laura Lewis, Rev. Wendy Lowe, Frederica Mathewes-Green, Andrea Mrozek, Lila Rose, Joni Eareckson Tada, and Patricia Wiedemer. I would be remiss in not recognizing other remarkable pro-women, pro-life advocates.[51]

---

49) Therese Hesketh and Zhu Wei Xing, "Abnormal sex ratios in human populations: Causes and consequences," Proceedings of the National Academy of Sciences 103(36), (September 5, 2006): 13271-13275, https://doi.org/10.1073/pnas.0602203103.

50) Marcelo Urquia et al., "Sex Ratios as Birth after Induced Abortion," *Canadian Medical Association Journal* 188(9), (June 2016): e181-e190.

51) Merle Baker, Ginimi Chan, Sherry Chan, Norma Cody, Stephanie Gray Connors, Angie Côté, Lorna Dueck, Lynn DuMerton, Christine Mackay, Patricia Maloney, Beth Moore, Camille Pauley, Nancy Pearcey, Rebecca Peters, Valerie Protopapas, Monica Roddis, Barbara Schmidt, Michele Smillie, Faye Sonier, Natalie Sonnen, Karen Stafford, Anna Marie White, and Doreen Yung.

IMPERFECTIONS

Termination of pregnancy for fetal abnormality (TOPFA) is legal in 113 countries.[52] Canada, the most permissive Western nation for TOPFA, permits such abortion for any serious and non-serious reason. Or for no reason. In contrast to Canada, many countries permit TOPFA only in instances where a life-threatening fetal abnormality will mean that the baby cannot be viable outside the womb.

In the United Kingdom, TOPFA can also be permissible where "the child, if born, would suffer physical or mental abnormalities that would result in serious handicap."[53] The seriousness of a handicap is considered on a case-by-case basis. However, with no legal definitions for "non- serious" neonatal conditions

52) Suzanne Heaney, Mark Tomlinson and Áine Aventin, "Termination of pregnancy for fetal anomaly: a systematic review of the healthcare experiences and needs of parents," *BMC Pregnancy Childbirth* 22, 441 (2022), https://bmcpregnancy childbirth.biomedcentral.com/articles/10.1186/s12884-022-04770-4.

53) Catherine Peckham et al., *Termination of Pregnancy for Fetal Abnormality in England, Scotland and Wales: Report of a Working Party,* Royal College of Obstetricians and Gynaecologists, May 2010, viii, https://www.rcog.org.uk/media/21lfvl0e/terminationpregnancyreport-18may2010.pdf.

in the *United Kingdom Abortion Act,* slippery slope abuses occur, including babies even having a cleft lip.[54]

Today, the most devalued babies (in addition to females) are those with Down syndrome, or Trisomy 21. Fetuses known or suspected to have Down syndrome are routinely terminated. In some Canadian provinces, nearly 85% of preborn children having Down syndrome are aborted. In the United Kingdom, almost 90%. Denmark, 98%. Iceland, virtually 100%.[55] As

---

54) The Right to Life Charitable Trust, "94% of Belgian doctors surveyed support 'after-birth abortion' for babies with disabilities," *Right to Life News,* United Kingdom, August 10, 2020, https://righttolife.org.uk/news/94-of-belgian-doctors-surveyed-support-after-birth-abortion-for-babies-with-disabilities.

55) Greg Angel, "Countries eliminate Down syndrome through abortion," *CBS News,* August 16, 2017.

actress Patricia Heaton, Honorary Chair of Feminists for Life, deplores, "Iceland isn't actually eliminating Down syndrome. They're just killing everybody that has it."[56]

INFANTS ARE NOT PERSONS

> *Thousands of medical ethicists and bioethicists, as they are called, professionally guide the unthinkable on its passage through the debatable on the way to becoming the justifiable until it is finally established as unexceptionable.*[57]

Some years ago, I had the opportunity to meet with human rights speaker, Melissa Ohden. Melissa had been born alive during a failed saline abortion and left for dead among discarded medical waste at a hospital in Ohio. She was later rescued by a nurse who heard her whimpers.

---

56) Patricia Heaton, "Patricia Heaton: 'Iceland isn't eliminating Down syndrome—they are just killing everyone who has it,'" *America: The Jesuit Review*, December 4, 2017, https://www.americamagazine.org/politics-society/2017/12/04/patricia-heaton-iceland-isnt-eliminating-down-syndrome-they-are-just.

57) Richard John Neuhaus, "The Return of Eugenics," *Commentary*, April 1988, https://www.commentary.org/articles/richard-neuhaus/the-return-of-eugenics/.

According to many prominent atheists, all babies, even after their birth, have "no moral right" to life. These physicians and "ethicists" are arguing for the legalization of infanticide for newborns with a disability, morbidity, or having survived an intended abortion. They include Drs. Michael Tooley, Jerry Coyne, Francesco Minerva, Alberto Giubilini, Peter Singer, and Helga Kuhse.

Jacqueline Laing summarizes Giubilini and Minerva's pro-infanticide position: "According to these related ideas [of personism and actualism], human beings achieve their moral status in virtue of the degree to which they are capable of laying value upon their lives or exhibiting certain qualities or being desirable to third-party family members."[58] This proposed practice—by means of exposure or euthanizing—is termed an "after-birth abortion" or "fourth-trimester abortion."

Our contemporary West has moved decidedly away from baseline moral absolutes (inherent with Judeo-Christian belief) to postmodern moral relativism. Christian ethicist Peter Kreeft observes that this worldview says that "only some humans are persons,

---

58) Jacqueline Laing, "Infanticide: A Reply to Giubilini and Minerva," abstract, *Journal of Medical Ethics* 39(5), (May 2013): 336-340.

for those who are given rights by others (that is, by those in power)."[59] Consequently, Kreeft laments, "'Hard pro-choice' denies the sanctity or inviolability of all humans; 'soft pro-choice' denies the humanity of the fetus."[60]

An example of this ever-increasing, non-inviolability belief is reflected in a recent 2020 poll. This survey revealed that 9 out of 10 Belgian nurses and physicians believe it to be morally permissible to

59) Peter Kreeft, *Three Approaches to Abortion: A Thoughtful and Compassionate Guide to Today's Most Controversial Issue* (San Francisco: Ignatius Press, 2002), 33.

60) Peter Kreeft, "Human Personhood Begins at Conception," accessed May 5, 2023, https://peterkreeft.com/topics-more/personhood.htm.

perform infanticide on newly born infants having a serious but non-lethal neonatal condition.[61]

Australian bioethicists Francesca Minerva and Alberto Giubilini go further. That is, to be able to legally euthanize perfectly healthy infants, since "newborns do not have the same moral status as actual persons."[62] According to Minerva and Giubilini, "What we call 'after-birth abortion' (killing a newborn) should be permissible in all the cases … including cases where the newborn is not disabled."[63]

Renowned American ethicist Peter Singer agrees. As Singer contends, "Since neither a newborn infant nor a fish is a person, the wrongness of killing such beings is not as great as the wrongness of killing a person."[64]

---

61) Ellen Roets et al., "Healthcare professionals' attitudes towards termination of pregnancy at viable stage," *Acta Obstetricia et Gynecologica Scandinavica* 100(1), (January 2021): 74-83, accessed May 27, 2023, https://obgyn.onlinelibrary.wiley.com/ doi/full/10.1111/aogs.13967.

62) Alberto Giubilini and Francesca Minerva, "After-birth abortion: Why should the baby live?," abstract, *Journal of Medical Ethics* 39(5), (May 2013): 261–263.

63) Giubilini and Minerva, "After-birth abortion," abstract. The bracketed "killing a newborn" is not added by me.

64) Peter Singer, *Rethinking Life and Death* (New York: St. Martin's Press, 1994), 220. Singer explains on his website why "killing a newborn baby is never equivalent to killing a person." See FAQ #9, accessed May 3, 2023, https://petersinger.info/faq.

We are back to the many past lived realities of the pre-Judeo-Christian world. Abortion is again commonplace. At particular risk again are preborn baby girls and infants with imperfections. In fact, any “unwanted” preborn baby is at risk for a host of explanations.

CHAPTER FOUR

ABORTION IN NORTH AMERICA TODAY

GRAVE STATISTICS

In Canada and the US, nearly 50% of all pregnancies are unintended.[65] Up to 95% of these women and their partners were inconsistent in using birth control

---

65) Society of Obstetricians and Gynaecologists of Canada, "Unintended Pregnancy," accessed May 5, 2023, https://pregnancy info.ca/your-pregnancy/special-consideration/unintended-pregnancy/. Megan Nichole Poole and Alana Cattapan, "The Unintended Outcomes of Mis-Measuring Unintended Pregnancies," *Canadian Bioethics, Law and Policy*, Memorial University Centre for Bioethics (June 2021), accessed August 2, 2023, https://impactethics.ca/2021/06/03/the-unintended-outcomes-of-mis-measuring-unintended-pregnancies.

or choosing not to use pregnancy prevention.[66] Centers for Disease Control recently revealed that unmarried women accounted for 86% of abortions. Adolescent girls (ages 15–19) for 8.5% and girls under 15 for 0.2%.[67]

Such unintended pregnancies will be happily or ambivalently carried to term, or will be aborted (37% in Canada, 42% in the US).[68] Adoption remains an unpopular alternative, with only 1% of women choosing this pregnancy option.[69]

Agencies no longer collect national adoption data. In Canada, women who chose adoption for their unexpected children was 5% in 1981, and 2% in

---

66) No birth control at 54%; inconsistent birth control at 41%. Luu D. Ireland, "Who are the 1 in 4 American women who choose abortion?," University of Massachusetts Chan Medical School, posted May 30, 2019, https://www.umassmed.edu/news/news-archives/2019/05/who-are-the-1-in-4-american-women-who-choose-abortion.

67) "U.S. Abortion Statistics", Abort73.com, accessed March 15, 2023, https://abort73.com/abortion_facts/us_abortion_ statistics/, citing Guttmacher Institute; "Canadian Abortion Statistics," accessed March 15, 2023, https://abort73.com/abortion_facts/canadian_abortion_statistics/, citing Canadian Institute for Health Information.

68) "Unintended Pregnancy and Abortion," Country Profile: Canada, Guttmacher Institute, accessed May 15, 2023, https://www.guttmacher.org/regions/northern-america/canada. U.S. statistic from Dr. Ireland, "Who are the 1 in 4?"

69) K.J. Daly and M.P. Sobol, "Adoption in Canada: Canadian Social Trends," *Child Welfare* 74(3), (May 1995): 665-677.

1989, the last known figure. With abortion clinics more accessible over the last 35 years, the assumed adoption estimates are 1%.

In the United States, women who chose adoption was approximately 9% prior to 1973. By the mid-1980s, adoption dropped to 2%. Then down to barely 1% in 2020 (the final year of captured data by the CDC).[70]

Many believe that terminating a pregnancy will be less painful emotionally than giving their child to adoptive parents.

Surveys are often extrapolations. But generally speaking, there are five primary reasons for choosing abortion, this according to women having had an abortion: timing (25%); finances (23%); not wanting a child or an additional child (19%); not in a committed relationship or in a bad relationship (8%); and feeling too young or not mature enough (7%).[71]

---

70) Olga Khazan, "Why So Many Women Choose Abortion Over Adoption," *The Atlantic*, May 20, 2019. https://www.theatlantic.com/health/archive/2019/05/why-more-women-dont-choose-adoption/589759/.

71) Ireland, "Who are the 1 in 4?" Statistical estimates are often extrapolated from limited, voluntary surveys, as were these figures from the CDC and Guttmacher Institute. "Reported Induced Terminations of Pregnancy by Reason, by Trimester," Agency for Health Care Administration (Florida), May 9, 2022, https://ahca.myflorida.com/mchq/central_services/training_support/docs/TrimesterByReason_2021.pdf.

Some 1 in 4 Canadian and American women will have one or more abortions during her lifetime.[72] Women having repeat abortions account for 34% in Canada and 42% in the US.[73]

The Canadian Institute for Health Information stopped reporting repeat abortions with its 2020 figures. The estimate of one-third is derived by culling past submissions from most, but not all, reporting hospitals. Abortion clinics in Canada do not disclose repeat abortion statistics.

BEHIND THE STATISTICS

Although abortion has become commonplace, please know this reality does not negate difficult, soul-searching, often traumatic pressures women can face when struggling to decide whether to abort or to

---

72) Sheila Dunn and Rebecca Cook, "Medical abortion in Canada: Behind the times," *Canadian Medical Association Journal* 186(1), (January 2014), 13. In fact, Dunn and Cook reference abortion provider Wendy Norman who suggests that one in three Canadian women will procure at least one abortion. See Wendy Norman, "Induced abortion in Canada 1974-2005," *Contraception* 85(2), (February 2012): 185-91; and Ireland, "Who are the 1 in 4?"

73) US statistic from Abort73.com, "U.S. Abortion Statistics." Canadian statistic of "one-third" in Kathryn J. LaRoche and Angel M. Foster, "Exploring Canadian Women's Multiple Abortion Experiences: Implications for Reducing Stigma and Improving Patient-Centered Care," *Women's Health Issues* 28(4), (July-August 2018): 327-332.

carry. Every year in Canada and the United States, tens of thousands of distressed, conflicted women and teen girls reach out to pregnancy care centres for information and help.

Many of these women believe that abortion is their only option due to significant and weighty stressors. These genuine obstacles may include the prospect of single parenthood, an interruption of education or career, financial hardship, or the lack of family support. Women often report being pressured into an unwanted abortion. Many women also come to these pregnancy centres seeking after-abortion care.

UNWANTED ABORTIONS

Untold numbers of women feel forced by others to have an abortion. In a Canadian study with one hundred post-abortion participants, two-thirds of these women said they were pressured or coerced into having their abortion.[74]

Pressure often takes the form of the boyfriend or partner threatening to leave the relationship. Being pushed by parents into an abortion is also frequently

---

74) Anne Broen et al., "Reasons for induced abortion and their relation to women's emotional distress," *General Hospital Psychiatry* 27(1), (February 2005): 36-43.

identified. Such women who are pressured by their partners or families are more likely to experience negative emotional reactions to abortion.[75]

Coercion is even more severe. One example: the parents who threatened to disavow their daughter because their grandbaby was of a mixed race. In this case, the young woman still chose to carry her child to term, even though the parents did, in fact, shun their daughter.

Another example: a husband who threatened his wife that if she did not procure an abortion, he would beat

75) David Reardon and Tessa Longbons, "Effects of Pressure to Abort on Women's Emotional Responses and Mental Health," abstract, *Cureus* 15(1), (January 31, 2023): e34456, doi:10.7759/cureus.34456.

her until she miscarried. He had done so before. On the very day his wife was going to commit suicide, she perchance heard about the help of a pregnancy care centre in her community. On that day, two lives were saved.[76]

POST-ABORTION STRESS

After an abortion, many women feel relief, while others have negative emotions. Reactions may be immediate, or the feelings may come up years later. Responses vary. They depend on a woman's age, stage of pregnancy, religious or cultural beliefs, previous mental health, or whether others are pressuring her into having an abortion.[77]

From a 2023 study, women who experience pressure from partners, family members, employers, or healthcare providers, "reported more negative emotions; more disruption of daily life, work, or

---

76) Case examples provided by the Crisis Pregnancy Centres of Burnaby and Vancouver, British Columbia.

77) Paragraph verbatim from Ginimi Chan, Brian Norton, Adrienne Mugwanya, and Musu Kanu Taylor-Lewis, *Abortion Parenting Adoption: an informational guide for unexpected pregnancy* (Red Deer, AB: Pregnancy Care Canada, 2020), 5, sourcing Canadian abortion providers (references available on request).

relationships."[78] Women who experience negative emotions convey the following reactions: sadness, guilt or shame, emotional numbing, depression, nightmares, thoughts of self-harm, and alcohol or drug abuse.[79]

For women with prolonged, unabated negative feelings, healthcare physicians recommend seeking lay or professional help.[80]

HOW SHALL WE THEN LIVE?

Pray. Speak out. Help out.

Here are some challenging words from our "conservative" sister in Christ, Rev. Alveda King: "By our effort and example may God use us, as imperfect

---

78) Reardon and Longbons, "Effects of Pressure," see Discussion.

79) Priscilla Coleman, "Abortion and mental health: Quantitative synthesis and analysis of research published 1995-2009," *British Journal of Psychiatry* 199(3), (September 2011): 180-86; and D.M. Fergusson, J.L. Horwood, and Joseph Broden, "Abortion and mental health disorders," *British Journal of Psychiatry* 193(6), (December 2008): 444-451; and Natalie Mota, Margaret Burnett, and Jitender Sareen, "Associations between abortion, mental disorders, and suicidal behaviour in a nationally representative sample," *Canadian Journal of Psychiatry* 55(4) (April 2010): 239-247.

80) Sarah Marshall et al., "Abortion: Emotional Recovery," *BC HealthLink*, Government of British Columbia, June 16, 2021, https://www.healthlinkbc.ca/pregnancy-parenting/planning-your-pregnancy/ending-pregnancy/abortion-emotional-recovery.

vessels that we are, to bring an end to such ancient evils as infanticide, abortion, racism, and oppression."[81]

Similarly, here are challenging words from our "progressive" brother in Christ, Shane Claiborne: "As Red Letter Christians, we need to be pro-life from the womb to the tomb. Abortion and euthanasia, the death penalty[82] and war, poverty and health care—all of these are issues of life and death."[83]

Individually and collectively, let us advocate for the worth and welfare of all who are vulnerable, all who are at risk. This means influencing public opinion and securing just legislation. This means speaking out. This is our prophetic call.

---

81) Alveda King and La Verne Tolbert, eds., *Life at All Costs: An Anthology of Voices from 21st Century Black Prolife Leaders*, (Bloomington, Indiana: Xlibris Publishing, 2012), 35. Rev. King is the daughter of A.D. King and niece of Martin Luther King, Jr.

82) Capital punishment is a moot point in Canada but not so in 58 non-European countries and the United States. In 2022, some 883 executions were recorded from 20 countries (18 in the US). This total does not include China, North Korea, and Vietnam, as execution data are state secrets. "Executions Around the World, 2022," Death Penalty Information Center, Washington, DC, accessed August 2, 2023, https://deathpenaltyinfo.org/policy-issues/international/executions-around-the-world.

83) Shane Claiborne and Tony Campolo, "A Dialogue on What it Means to be Pro-Life," *Red Letter Christians*, web article, January 22, 2023, https://www.redletterchristians.org/a-dialogue-on-what-it-means-to-be-pro-life/.

Individually and collectively, let us open our hearts, our wallets, our homes, and our churches for women experiencing unexpected pregnancies and for isolated single parents in need. This means helping out. This is our pastoral call.

In sum, who will disagree with this earnest call to care from Francis Schaeffer and C. Everett Koop? "Merely to say …'You must not have an abortion'—without being ready to involve ourselves in the problem—is another way of being inhumane."[84]

Pray. Speak out. Help out.

Let us not grow weary doing works of love.

For considerations specific to helping women experiencing unexpected pregnancies, see Appendix A, "Pregnancy Care Centres." For considerations specific to seeking legislative abortion restrictions in Canada and the United States, see Appendix B, "The Politics of Abortion."

84) C. Everett Koop and Francis Schaeffer, *Whatever Happened to the Human Race?* rev. ed. (Wheaton: Crossway Books, 1983), 73.

CHAPTER FIVE

CONCLUSION

Though some people may believe or wish otherwise, abortion is not and never has been a Christian conviction. Since the genesis of the Church, the Judeo-Christian belief has embodied universal human dignity. From antiquities historian Michael J. Gorman, "[Christians] pleaded for the poor, the weak, women, children and the unborn. This pro-life ethic discarded hate in favour of love, war in favour of peace, oppression in favour of justice, bloodshed in favour of life."[85]

May we, as God's adopted daughters and sons—Catholic, Orthodox, and Protestant—continue the

85) Gorman, *Abortion and the Early Church*, 90.

life-affirming legacy of the Church. This is to say, love them both: mother and child.

LORD, may your kingdom come. May your will be done on earth as it is in heaven.

APPENDIX A

PREGNANCY CARE CENTRES

> Being heard is so close to being loved that for the average person, they are almost indistinguishable. - Dr. David W. Augsburger

You may not be familiar with the unique faith-based ministry of pregnancy care centres, at times referred to as crisis pregnancy centres. Most pregnancy care centres in Canada are affiliated with the national best practice association, Pregnancy Care Canada. Most centres in the United States are affiliated with either Care Net or Heartbeat International.

These affiliates provide a safe environment for a woman to make a pregnancy decision that is fully informed, evidence-based, and free from external pressure. The staff and volunteers respect a woman's right to make her own decision and seek to provide her with medically accurate information on all three options: abortion, adoption, and parenting.

I appreciate these germane words from an affiliate of Pregnancy Care Canada:

> "If a client of our centre obtains an abortion, we love her. If she carries to term, we love her. If she releases a child in an adoption, we love her. If she grieves after the abortion, with zero judgment we will mourn with her. If she is in need during parenting, we will care for her. If she struggles after the adoption, we will support her."[86]

Additionally, most affiliates offer prenatal instruction, parenting classes, financial aid, material support (maternity/baby clothes, formula, diapers, furnishings), and after-abortion care. For women unable to access a local centre in their community, online support is also available with OnlineCare in Canada and OptionLine in the US. All services are available free of charge.

---

86) Interview with Crisis Pregnancy Centre of Winnipeg, in "Crisis Pregnancy Centres," *Growing Together*, Evangelical Mennonite Conference, August 23, 2022.

APPENDIX B

THE POLITICS OF ABORTION

> Morality, like art, means drawing a line somewhere. - G.K. Chesterton

In a pluralistic democracy, where should our elected legislators draw the line on abortion? What follows are possible legislative restrictions, all highly debated, all contentious.

At the *restrictive* end of the spectrum: a ban on abortion—unless the woman's life is at risk. Some, but not all, pro-life advocates will include pregnancies from rape and incest.

A former abortion provider informed me that after becoming a Christian he stopped performing abortions even if the woman's life could be at risk. With patient permission, he closely monitors her health and, when it becomes necessary, induces labour, thus purposing to save two lives. (If a patient is uncomfortable with such a plan, he refers the patient to another doctor.) Sometimes, the preemie babies are too young to survive. Other times, the babies thrive.

At the *permissive* end of the spectrum: abortion on demand. Thus, abortion to be sanctioned for any reason, for no reason, up to the moment of birth.

Within the restrictive-permissive spectrum, most Canadians and Americans advocate for a set legal limit at a particular stage of fetal development. Some such examples: when a heartbeat is detected (~6 weeks after gestation);[87] to the end of 15 weeks; or 24 weeks; or to the end of the second trimester.

---

87) Valinda Nwadike, "How Early Can You Hear Baby's Heartbeat on Ultrasound and By Ear?," *Healthline*, September 26, 2018, https://www.healthline.com/health/pregnancy/when-can-you-hear-babys-heartbeat.

Beyond the spectrum, various high-profile bioethicists are advocating legalized infanticide.[88] Taking the life of infants who are born is to be regarded as a "fourth-trimester abortion" or an "after-birth abortion." This proposed practice (via exposure or euthanizing) to be made permissible with newborns having an infirmity, or having survived an abortion.[89] Some such atheist ethicists even advocate for legalized infanticide of perfectly healthy unwanted newborns.[90]

On this side of heaven, we will never reach a consensus where an ethical line is to be drawn in respecting a woman's bodily autonomy and protection for the unborn. In our broken world, what can we do *at least*?

This is what we know. A majority of Americans and Canadian support restrictions on abortion.

---

88) Drs. Michael Tooley, Jerry Coyne, Francesco Minerva, Alberto Giubilini, Peter Singer, Helga Kuhse, and others.

89) As shared in Chapter 3, I had the opportunity to meet with human rights activist, Melissa Ohden. She had been born alive during a failed saline abortion and left for dead among an Ohio hospital's discarded medical waste. Melissa was later rescued by a nurse who heard her whimpers.

90) Giubilini and Minerva, "After-birth abortion," abstract. Singer, *Rethinking Life and Death,* 220. See *Being Human*, Chapter 3, subheading "Infants Are Not Persons," beginning on page 36.

From a recent US national poll:

> Two in three Americans want significant restrictions placed on abortion. 66% say abortion should only be allowed, at most, within the first three months during pregnancy. 34% say abortion should be permitted during the first six months of pregnancy or at any time. Most Republicans (86%) and independents (73%) favor restricting abortion to, at most, the first trimester of pregnancy. While a majority of Democrats (58%) favor a longer window for abortions to be performed, even 42% of Democrats want limitations.[91]

Restriction beliefs held by Canadians: Many desire a one or two-day "second-thoughts" waiting period; a law requiring doctors to inform patients on the "alternatives to abortion" (78%); and a law requiring patients to be informed on the "risks of abortion"

91) From "Abortion Rights in the United States," NPR/PBS News-Hour/Marist National Poll, April 26, 2023, https://maristpoll.marist.edu/polls/abortion-rights-in-the-united-states.

(93%).[92] Further, in a recent (2020) Dart poll, nearly half of the respondents oppose second-trimester abortion and 70% want third-trimester abortion to be illegal.[93] These convictions are consistent with other Canadian polls.

We need to be discerning with polls. How a question is framed will influence an answer. A good example is the Dart survey: "In that poll, 71% believe a woman should be able to get an abortion *for any reason*, but at the same time 70% of Canadians think abortion *should be illegal* in the last trimester, and 84% said they supported a law against sex selective abortion."[94] (Emphasis mine.)

In Canada, there are no gestational legal limits on abortion. We have no abortion law whatsoever. "The last Canadian abortion law was struck down in 1988 making abortion up until birth legal in Canada.

---

92) "Canadian Opinions on Abortion: Abortion Polls Summarized," We Need a Law, June 4, 2020, https://weneedalaw.ca/2020/06/canadian-opinions-on-abortion. These statistics are citing the Dart survey.

93) We Need a Law, *Canadian Opinions.*

94) We Need a Law, *Canadian Opinions.* The WNL organization continues: "There is a difference between being asked 'Do you support women [to have abortions]?' versus 'Do you support the termination of a 24-week old fetus who is viable and can feel pain?'"

There is no legal right to abortion; what exists is an absence of laws restricting abortion."[95]

While I was seeking research data for this appendix, there was a celebratory national story: the one-year anniversary when a Toronto hospital heroically saved the lives of preemie twins born at 22 weeks.[96] Yet, a month earlier, there had been another national story: a Montreal hospital aborted a viable, full-term 38-week gestation baby.[97] Madness.

In the United States, restrictions vary widely from state to state. Examples at the time of this writing: 12 states ban abortion (exc. when a woman's life at risk; some including also for rape). No gestational

---

95) Laura Lewis, "Canada in a Post Roe v. Wade Era," Pregnancy Care Canada (blog), June 21, 2022, https://pregnancycarecanada.ca/canada-in-a-post-roe-v-wade-era/. See *R v. Morgentaler*, Case No. 19556, Supreme Court of Canada, 1988.

96) "'0% chance of survival': Ontario twins born at 22 weeks beat the odds and set world record," *National Post*, published March 7, 2023, https://nationalpost.com/news/twins-set-record-for-most-premature-birth.

97) Faytene Grasseschi, "Parliament's Return: Overshadowed by Disturbing Abortion in Montreal," 4my Canada, e-communication, February 3, 2023, https://madmimi.com/s/76eb851.

restrictions in 6 states. Most states have set limits (e.g. 15 weeks, 22 weeks, 24 weeks, or viability).[98]

In addition, 24 US states require a 24-hour wait period; 17 states require state-mandated counselling; and 12 states require the patient to be informed of the possibility of a fetus experiencing abortion-procedure pain. Further, 36 states require parental consent for minors, and 21 states prohibit "partial-birth" abortion.[99] Post *Dobbs v. Jackson*,[100] various state governments are re-evaluating their respective abortion policies.

One thing is not in dispute. Most Canadians and Americans (and Europeans) are not in favour of unrestricted abortion during all stages of fetal gestation.[101]

---

98) Guttmacher Institute, "State Laws and Policies: An Overview of Abortion Laws," accessed May 3, 2023, https://www. guttmacher.org/state-policy/explore/overview-abortion-laws.

99) Guttmacher Institute, "State Laws and Policies."

100) Supreme Court of the United States, 19-1392 *Dobbs v. Jackson Women's Health Organization*, June 24, 2022.

101) Consider reading the findings from the largest study of American attitudes toward abortion, in Dr. Tricia Bruce et al., *How Americans Understand Abortion*, McGrath Institute, University of Notre Dame, 2020.

Below are the legislative abortion standards for European countries with similar national political and judicial institutions.[102]

AN OVERVIEW OF ABORTION LAWS

	WAITING PERIOD (DAYS)	COUNSELING	GESTATIONAL LIMIT (WEEKS)
Belgium	6	✓	12
Canada	-	-	-
Denmark	-	✓	12
Finland	-	✓	20
Germany	3	✓	12
Iceland	-	✓	16
Italy	7	-	12
Netherlands	6	✓	24
Norway	-	✓	12
United Kingdom	-	-	24
Portugal	3	-	12
Spain	3	-	14
Sweden	-	-	18
Switzerland	-	✓	12

102) Pictograph used with permission from We Need a Law, "International Standards Abortion Law," accessed October 3, 2023, https://weneedalaw.ca/initiatives/international-standards-abortion-law/.

APPENDIX C

CONSISTENT LIFE ETHIC RESOURCES

> Being pro-life means viewing every life with unconditional love and kindness. - Kirstie Piper[103]

Being Human is written from a Judeo-Christian perspective on the ethics of abortion and caring for women experiencing unexpected pregnancies. But, of course, there are pro-life organizations which are not necessarily Christian. Quoting from one such secular group, "You do not have to be religious to value

103) Kirstie Piper is a writer, director, and producer specializing in humanitarian and faith-based content.

human life. You do not have to be religious to see the humanity of the fetus."

Diverse pro-women, pro-life organizations in North America include:

- Artists for Life
- Association for Medical Ethics
- Birthright
- Canadian Physicians for Life
- deVeber Institute for Bioethics and Social Policy
- Elliot Institute
- Evangelical Fellowship of Canada
- Feminists for Life of America
- Focus On The Family
- International Black Women's Network
- Jewish Pro-Life Foundation
- Life Canada National
- National Campus Life Network
- National Legal Foundation
- Nurses for Life
- Project Rachel
- ProWomanProLife
- RightNow
- The AND (&) Campaign
- Women Exploited by Abortion
- Women for Human Rights

Many life-affirming organizations provide direct client care. Some are educational, others are political, and yet others, activist.

If of interest, you may wish to acquaint yourself with the Consistent Life Network, an association of over 200 international humanitarian organizations working to curb abortion, infanticide, poverty, racism, capital punishment, and war. Rehumanize International is a secular global network of peacemakers opposing abortion, infanticide, torture, unjust war, police brutality, and the death penalty.

Regarding overt activist groups, this includes Live Action, a politically non-partisan organization which conducts investigations of unethical practices by abortion providers. Warning: Live Action posts distressing content and images.

On the far-left, the Progressive Anti-Abortion Uprising is a feminist, 2SLGBTQIA+ identifying, anti-capitalism, pro-life organization. The leadership includes self-described atheists, socialists, anarcho mutualists, and communists. According to this group, "Abortion does not disappear societal problems; it disappears human beings."[104]

---

104) "Stances: Capitalism," Progressive Anti-Abortion Uprising, accessed July 30, 2023, https://paaunow.org/stances-capitalism.

If you wish to know about Christian international ministries which embrace a consistent life ethic, here are some examples:

- Caritas Internationalis
- Catholic Climate Covenant
- Evangelical Environment Network
- Heartbeat International
- International Orthodox Christian Charities
- MaterCare International
- Missionaries of Charity
- Samaritan's Purse International
- The Salvation Army International
- World Evangelical Alliance
- World Vision International

Here are official statements from two of the aforementioned ministries:

WORLD VISION STATEMENT

> *World Vision is pro-life. We believe that life begins at conception, and World Vision does not provide, recommend, or refer women for abortions or methods of birth control that are proven to be abortifacient.*[105]

---

105) World Vision International, "2018 International Conference on Family Planning," August 2, 2023, https://www.worldvision.org/our-work/health/icfp2018.

SALVATION ARMY STATEMENT

The Salvation Army accepts the moment of fertilization as the start of human life. We believe that society has a responsibility to care for others, and especially to protect and promote the welfare of vulnerable people, including unborn children. The Salvation Army believes that life is a gift from God and we are answerable to God for the taking of life.[106]

---

106) The Salvation Army International, "Positional Statement: Abortion," High Council of The Salvation Army, November 2010, accessed July 19, 2023, https://www.salvationarmy.org/ihq/ipsabortion.

BIBLIOGRAPHY

Abort73.com. "Canadian Abortion Statistics." Accessed March 15, 2023. https://abort73.com/abortion_facts/canadian_ abortion_statistics/.

Abort73.com. "U.S. Abortion Statistics." Accessed March 15, 2023. https://abort73.com/ abortion_facts/us_abortion_ statistics/.

"Abortion Rights in the United States." NPR/PBS NewsHour/Marist National Poll. April 26, 2023. https://maristpoll.marist.edu/polls/abortion-rights-in-the-united-states/.

Agency for Health Care Administration. "Reported Induced Terminations of Pregnancy (ITOP) by Reason, by Trimester." AHCA Florida website, May 9, 2022. https://ahca.myflorida.com/content/download/7207/file/Trimester ByReason_2021.pdf.

Ambrose, Augustus. *The Women of Gilead: The Abuse of Women and Children in History.* New York: Uptown Bookseller, 1957. Ambrose. *Hexameron.* c. AD 389.

Angel, Greg. "Countries eliminate Down syndrome through abortion." *CBS News*, August 16, 2017.

Antiochian Orthodox Church. "Writings from the Fathers on the Sacred Gift of Life." Englewood: Antiochian Orthodox Christian Archdiocese of North America, 2020.

Aquilina, Mike. *The Witness of Early Christian Women: Mothers of the Church.* Huntington: Our Sunday Visitor Publishing, 2014.

Aquinas, Thomas. *Summa Theologica.* c. AD 1265 to 1273.

Aristotle. *Historia Animalium.* c. 340 BC.

Aristotle. *Politics.* c. 350 BC.

Athenagoras. "The Christians Condemn and Detest All Cruelty." *A Plea Regarding Christians.* c. AD 177.

Augustine. *On Marriage and Concupiscence* (Book I). c. AD 401.

Barnabas. *Letter of Barnabas*, 19.5. Preserved in the 4th century *Codex Sinaiticus.*

Barth, Karl. *Church Dogmatics.* Translated by G.W. Bromiley and T.E. Torrance. Vol. 3, Pt. 4. Edinburgh: T & T Clark, 1961.

Basil. *Canonica Prima.* 188. c. AD 374.

Berić, Berislav and Nila Kapor-Stanulović. "The Greek Orthodox Church and position regarding birth control." *Contraception, Fertilité, Sexualité* 11(9), (September 1983): 1053-1055.

Bonhoeffer, Dietrich. *Ethics.* Translated by Neville Horton Smith. New York: Macmillan, 1955.

Bowman-Smart, Hilary, Julian Savulescu, Christopher Gyngell, Cara Mand, and Martin Delatycki. "Sex selection and non-invasive prenatal testing: A review of current practices, evidence, and ethical issues." *Prenatal Diagnosis* 40(4), (March 2020): 398-407.

Breck, John. *The Sacred Gift of Life: Orthodox Christianity and Bioethics.* Crestwood, NY: Saint Vladimir's Seminary Press, 1998.

Brind'Amour, Katherine. "St. Thomas Aquinas (c. 1225-1274)." In *The Embryo Project Encyclopedia.* Arizona State University, 2007. Accessed May 13, 2023. https://embryo.asu.edu/pages/st-thomas-aquinas-c-1225-1274.

Broen, Anne Nordal, Torbjörn Moum, Anne Sejersted Bödtker, and Ekeberg Øivind. "Reasons for induced abortion and their relation to women's emotional distress: A prospective, two-year follow-up study." *General Hospital Psychiatry* 27(1), (February 2005): 36-43.

Bruce, Tricia C., Bridget Ritz, Maureen Day, Kendra Hutchens, and Patricia Tevington. *How Americans Understand Abortion*. McGrath Institute, University of Notre Dame, 2020. Accessed May 13, 2023. https://news.nd.edu/assets/395804/how_americans_understand_abortion_final_7_15_20.pdf.

Calvin, John. *Commentaries on the Four Last Books of Moses.* Grand Rapids: Eerdmans, 1950.

Canadian Encyclopedia. "Early Women's Movements in Canada: 1867–1960." Historica Canada. Published August 15, 2016. https://www.thecanadianencyclopedia.ca/en/article/early-womens-movements-in-canada.

Canadian Encyclopedia. "Women's Movements in Canada: 1960–85." Historica Canada. Published September 12, 2016. https://www.thecanadianencyclopedia.ca/en/article/womens-movements-in-canada-196085.

Castelló, Adela, Marcelo Urquia, María Ángeles Rodríguez-Arenas, and Francisco Bolúmar. "Missing girls among deliveries from Indian and Chinese mothers in Spain 2007–2015," *European Journal of Epidemiology* 34(7), (March 2019): 699-709.

Chan, Ginimi, Adrienne Mugwanya, Brian Norton, and Musu Kanu Taylor-Lewis. *Abortion Parenting Adoption: an informational guide for unexpected pregnancy.* Red Deer, AB: Pregnancy Care Canada, 2020.

Chao, Fengqing, Patrick Gerland, Alkema Leontine, and Alex R. Cook. "Systematic assessment of the sex ratio at birth for all countries and estimation of national imbalances and regional reference levels." *Proceedings of the National Academy of Sciences of the United States* 116, no. 19 (April 2019): 9303-9311. https://doi.org/10.1073/pnas.1812593116.

Christians for Biblical Equality. "Women Leaders at the Table in Early Churches." *Priscilla Papers*, Volume 34, Number 2, Spring 2020.

Chrysostom. *Homilies on Romans.* 24. c. AD 392.

Churches of St. Paul and St. Michael. "Pro-Life Quotes." Worship. Zumbrota and Pine Island, Minnesota. Accessed August 2, 2023. https://www.stpaulstmichael.com/copy-of-prayers-reflections.

Claiborne, Shane, and Tony Campolo. "A Dialogue on What it Means to be Pro-Life." *Red Letter Christians.*

January 22, 2023. https://www.redletterchristians.org/a-dialogue-on-what-it-means-to-be-pro-life/.

Claiborne, Shane. *Rethinking Life: Embracing the Sacredness of Every Person.* Grand Rapids: Zondervan, 2023.

Clement of Alexandria. *Paedagogus*, Book III. c. AD 198.

Coleman, Priscilla, Kaitlyn Boswell, Katrina Etzkorn, and Rachel Turnwald. "Women who suffered emotionally from abortion: Qualitative synthesis of their experiences." *Journal of American Physicians and Surgeons* 22(4), (November 2017): 112-118.

Coleman, Priscilla. "Abortion and mental health: Quantitative synthesis and analysis of research published 1995-2009." *British Journal of Psychiatry* 199(3), (September 2011): 180-86.

Conlon, Mickey. "Feminists must 'reconcile with their roots'." *The Catholic Register (Toronto),* November 15, 2018.

Cyprian. *Novatus.* Epistle 48. c. AD 250.

Daly, Kerry J. and Michael P. Sobol. "Adoption in Canada: Canadian Social Trends." *Child Welfare.* Vol. 74, No. 3, 1995: 665-677.

Dawson, Myrna, Angelika Zecha, Haleakala Angus, Ciara Boyd, Emily Graham, Taylor Hendren, Abigail Mitchell et al. "Understanding sex/gender-related killings of women and girls in Canada, 2018–2022." University of Guelph: Canadian Femicide Observatory for Justice and Accountability, 2023.

Death Penalty Information Center. "Executions Around the World, 2022." DPIC website, Washington DC. Accessed August 2, 2023. https://deathpenaltyinfo.org/policy-issues/international/executions-around-the-world.

Derr, Mary Krane, Rachel MacNair, and Linda Naranjo-Huebl. *Prolife Feminism: Yesterday and Today.* Kansas City: Feminism and Nonviolence Studies Association, 2005. Quoted in Cat Clark, "The Truth About Susan B. Anthony," Feminists for Life of America. Accessed May 15, 2023, https://www.feministsforlife.org/the-truth-about-susan-b-anthony/.

Devereux, George. "A Typological Study of Abortion in 350 Primitive, Ancient, and Pre-Industrial Societies." In *Abortion in America: Medical, psychiatric, legal, anthropological, and religious considerations.* Edited by Harold Rosen. Boston: Beacon Press, 1967. Quoted in George Grant. *Grand Illusions: The Legacy of Planned Parenthood*, 2nd ed. Franklin: Adroit Press, 1992.

Didache. The Lord's Teaching Through the Twelve Apostles to the Nations. c. AD 80-90.

Dunn, Sheila, and Rebecca Cook. "Medical abortion in Canada: Behind the times." *Canadian Medical Association Journal* 186(1), (January 2014).

Ekeocha, Obianuju. *Target Africa: Ideological Neocolonialism of the Twenty-First Century*. San Francisco: Ignatius Press, 2018.

Evangelical Fellowship of Canada. "Sanctity of Life." Accessed May 5, 2023. https://www.evangelicalfellowship.ca/Themes /Sanctity-of-Life.

Fergusson, David M., John L. Horwood, and Joseph M. Broden. "Abortion and mental health disorders: Evidence from a 30-year longitudinal study." *British Journal of Psychiatry* 193(6), (December 2008): 444-451.

Foster, Serrin M., and Damian J. Geminder. "Erasing Margaret Sanger from Planned Parenthood doesn't change abortion's eugenic logic." *America: The Jesuit Review*, July 22, 2020. https://www.americamagazine.org/politics-society/2020/07/22/margaret-sanger-feminism-planned-parenthood-abortion-eugenics.

Foster, Serrin M. "Feminist Foremothers." Feminists for Life of America. Accessed May 15, 2023. https://www.feministsforlife.org/herstory/.

Foster, Serrin M. "Women Deserve Better than Abortion: The Ultimate Exploitation of Women." *National Review*, January 19, 2018. https://www.nationalreview.com/2018/01/womens-march-pro-life-feminists/.

Fowler, Paul B. *Abortion: Toward an Evangelical Consensus.* Portland: Multnomah Press, 1987.

Giubilini, Alberto, and Francesca Minerva. "After-birth abortion: Why should the baby live?" *Journal of Medical Ethics* 39(5), (May 2013): 261-263.

Gomez, José, Thomas Daly, Mario Dorsonville-Rodríguez, Andrew Cozzens, Paul Coakley, David Malloy, Salvatore Cordileone et al. "Standing with Moms in Need." United States Conference of Catholic Bishops, Washington DC, 2020.

Gorman, Michael J. *Abortion and the Early Church: Christian, Jewish, and Pagan Attitudes in the Greco-Roman World.* Eugene: Wipf and Stock Publishers, 1982.

Graham, Billy. "Billy Graham's Answers on Abortion." Billy Graham Evangelistic Association,

January 2022. https://billygraham.org/story/billy-grahams-answers-on-abortion/.

Grant, George. *Grand Illusions: The Legacy of Planned Parenthood.* 2nd ed. Franklin, TN: Adroit Press, 1992.

Grant, George. *Third Time Around: A History of the Pro-Life Movement from the First Century to the Present.* Brentwood, TN: Wolgemuth and Hyatt, 1991.

Grasseschi, Faytene. "Parliament's Return: Overshadowed by Disturbing Abortion in Montreal." 4my Canada. National Update online communication. February 3, 2023. https://madmimi.com/s/76eb851.

Gregory. "On the Soul and the Resurrection." *The Sacred Writings of Gregory of Nyssa.* Augsburg, Germany: Jazzybee Verlag, 2012.

Guttmacher Institute. "State Laws and Policies: An Overview of Abortion Laws." Accessed May 3, 2023. https://www.guttmacher.org/state-policy/explore/overview-abortion-laws.

Guttmacher Institute. "Unintended Pregnancy and Abortion." Country Profile: Canada. Accessed May 15, 2023. https://www.guttmacher.org/regions/northern-america/canada.

Heaney, Suzanne, Mark Tomlinson, and Áine Aventin. "Termination of pregnancy for fetal anomaly: a systematic review of the healthcare experiences and needs of parents." *BMC Pregnancy and Childbirth* 22:441 (May 26, 2022): 1-29. https://bmcpregnancychildbirth.biomedcentral.com/articles/10.1186/s12884-022-04770-4.

Heaton, Patricia. "Patricia Heaton: 'Iceland isn't eliminating Down syndrome—they are just killing everyone who has it.'" *America: The Jesuit Review.* December 4, 2017. https://www.americamagazine.org/politics-society/2017/12/04/patricia-heaton-iceland-isnt-eliminating-down-syndrome-they-are-just.

Hesketh, Therese, and Zhu Wei Xing. "Abnormal sex ratios in human populations: Causes and Consequences." *Proceedings of the National Academy of Sciences of the United States* 103, no.36 (September 5, 2006): 13271-5. https://doi.org/10.1073/pnas.0602203103.

Hippolytus. *Refutation of All Heresies.* Book 9. c. AD 225.

Holy Orthodox Church. "An Orthodox View of Abortion." *Brief Amicus Curiae of the Holy Orthodox Church.* Submitted to the Supreme Court of the United States. No. 88-605, February 21, 1989.

http://orthodoxkansas.org/Orthodox_Amicus_Curiae_brief.html.

Hui, Edwin, ed. *Questions of Right and Wrong: The Proceedings of the 1993 Clinical Bioethics Conference.* Vancouver: Regent College, 1994.

Hurtado, Larry. *Destroyer of the gods: Early Christian Distinctiveness in the Roman World.* Waco: Baylor University Press, 2016.

Ireland, Luu D. "Who are the 1 in 4 American women who choose abortion?" University of Massachusetts Chan Medical School. Posted May 30, 2019. https://www.umassmed.edu/news/news-archives/2019/05/who-are-the-1-in-4-american-women-who-choose-abortion.

Jerome. *Letter to Eustochium.* XXII. c. AD 390-404.

Johnson, Alexis McGill. "I'm the Head of Planned Parenthood. We're Done Making Excuses for Our Founder: We must reckon with Margaret Sanger's association with white supremacist groups and eugenics." *New York Times*, April 17, 2021. https://www.nytimes.com/2021/04/17/opinion/planned-parenthood-margaret-sanger.html.

Khazan, Olga. "Why So Many Women Choose Abor-tion Over Adoption." *The Atlantic.* May 20, 2019.

King, Alveda, and Tolbert, La Verne, eds., *Life at All Costs: An Anthology of Voices from 21st Century Black Prolife Leaders*. Bloomington, Indiana: Xlibris Publishing, 2012.

Koop, C. Everett, and Francis Schaeffer. *Whatever Happened to the Human Race?* rev. ed. Wheaton: Crossway Books, 1983.

Kornelsen, Dallas. "Crisis Pregnancy Centres." Interview by Erica Fehr. *Growing Together*. Evangelical Mennonite Conference. August 23, 2022. https://www.emcmessenger.ca/growing-together/crisis-pregnancy-centres-what-we-stand-to-lose.

Kowalczyk, John. *An Orthodox View of Abortion.* Minneapolis: Gopher State Litho, 1977.

Kreeft, Peter. "Human Personhood Begins at Conception." Accessed May 5, 2023. https://peterkreeft.com/topics-more/personhood.htm.

Kreeft, Peter. *Three Approaches to Abortion: A Thoughtful and Compassionate Guide to Today's Most Controversial Issue.* San Francisco: Ignatius Press, 2002.

Kreider, Alan. *The Patient Ferment of the Early Church.* Grand Rapids: Baker Academic, 2016.

Laing, Jaqueline A. "Infanticide: A Reply to Giubilini and Minerva." *Journal of Medical Ethics* 39(5), (2013): 336-340.

Lanfranchi, Angela, Ian Gentles, and Elizabeth Ring-Cassidy. *Complications: Abortion's Impact on Women.* Toronto: deVeber Institute for Bioethics and Social Research, 2013.

LaRoche, Kathryn J. and Angel M. Foster. "Exploring Canadian Women's Multiple Abortion Experiences: Implications for Reducing Stigma and Improving Patient-Centered Care." *Women's Health Issues* 28(4), (July-August 2018): 327-332.

Lewis, Laura. "Canada in a Post Roe v. Wade Era." *Pregnancy Care Canada*, blog, June 21, 2022. https://pregnancycarecanada.ca/canada-in-a-post-roe-v-wade-era/.

Lewis, Laura. *More Than One Choice: How to Love and Support an Unexpected Pregnancy*. Independently published. 2024. Available from Amazon.ca.

Libreria Editrice Vaticana, *Catechism of the Catholic Church.* Washington DC: United States Conference of Catholic Bishops, 2008.

Luther, Martin. *What Luther Says: An Anthology.* Compiled by Ewald M. Plass. Vol. 2, No. 2826. St. Louis: Concordia Publishing House, 1959.

Mares, Courtney. "Pope Francis decries culture that 'throws away' unborn children, elderly, poor," *Catholic News Agency,* Vatican City, January 29, 2023.

Marshall, Sarah, Anne C. Poinier, Adam Husney Kathleen Romito, Rebecca H. Allen, Kirtly Jones, and Femi Olatunbosun. "Abortion: Emotional Recovery." *BC HealthLink*, Government of British Columbia, June 16, 2021.https://www.healthlinkbc.ca/pregnancy-parenting/planning-your-pregnancy/ending-pregnancy/abortion-emotional-recovery.

Mathetes. *Letter of Mathetes to Diognetus.* Chapter 5: "The Manners of the Christians."

Mathewes-Green, Frederica. "The Pro-Life Cause, Orthodoxy, and Hope." Ancient Faith Ministries. January 12, 2012. https://blogs.ancientfaith.com/blogs/.

Mattingly, Toikerry. "Hard To Avoid Religion When Fighting About Fourth-Trimester Abortions," *Religion Unplugged*, February 15, 2019.

McConnell, Michael W. "Religion and the Search for a Principled Middle Ground on Abortion." *Michigan Law Review* 92(6), (May 1994): 1893-1909. Accessed May 15, 2023. https://repository.law.umich.edu/mlr/vol92/iss6/36.

McLaughlin, Rebecca. *Jesus Through the Eyes of Women.* La Grange: The Gospel Coalition, 2022.

Mensch, Elizabeth, and Alan Freeman. *The Politics of Virtue: Is Abortion Debatable?* Durham: Duke University Press, 1993.

Miller, Matt. "How the Evangelical Church Awoke to the Abortion Issue," Alliance of Confessing Evangelicals, Reformation21, March 4, 2013.

Minucius Felix, Marcus. *Octavius.* c. AD 197.

Mota, Natalie, Margaret Burnett, and Jitender Sareen. "Associations between abortion, mental disorders, and suicidal behaviour in a nationally representative sample." *Canadian Journal of Psychiatry* 55(4), (April 2010): 239-47.

Mrozek, Andrea. "Celebrating Women." *Cardus.* Last modified March 8, 2017. https://www.cardus.ca/news/news-releases/celebrating-women/.

Mrozek, Andrea. "Women's Happiness, Women's Health: The Feminist Fight Against Abortion." *Cardus.* Last modified March 4, 2019. https://www.cardus.ca/research/family/research-report/womens-happiness-womens-health/.

National Health Service United Kingdom. "You and your baby at 24 weeks pregnant." October

13, 2021. https://www.nhs.uk/pregnancy/week-by-week/13-to-27/24-weeks/.

National Post. "'0% chance of survival': Ontario twins born at 22 weeks beat the odds and set world record." Published March 7, 2023. https://nationalpost.com/news/twins-set-record-for-most-premature-birth.

Neuhaus, Richard John. "The Return of Eugenics." *Commentary*. April 1988. https://www.commentary.org/articles/richard-neuhaus/the-return-of-eugenics/.

Norman, Wendy. "Induced abortion in Canada 1974–2005: Trends over the first generation with legal access." *Contraception* 85(2), (February 2012): 185-191.

Nwadike, Valinda. "How Early Can You Hear Baby's Heartbeat on Ultrasound and By Ear?" *Healthline*. September 26, 2018. https://www.healthline.com/health/pregnancy/when-can-you-hear-babys-heart-beat. Origen. *Contra Celsum*. 3.61-62.

Peckham, Catherine, Kay Ellis, Jane Fisher, Bertie Leigh, Judith Schott, Tahir Mahmood, Neil Marlow et al. *Termination of Pregnancy for Fetal Abnormality in England, Scotland, and Wales: Report of a Working Party*. Royal College of Obstetricians and Gynaecologists. May 2010. Accessed March 23, 2023. https://

www.rcog.org.uk/media/21lfvl0e/terminationpregnancyreport18may2010.pdf.

Photius. *Photian Collection.* AD 883.

Plato. *The Republic*, Book V. c. 375 BC.

Poole, Megan Nichole, and Alana Cattapan. "The Unintended Outcomes of Mis-Measuring Unintended Pregnancies." *Canadian Bioethics, Law, and Policy.* St. John's, NL: Memorial University, 2021. Accessed August 2, 2023. https://impactethics.ca/2021/06/03/the-unintended-outcomes-of-mis-measuring-unintended-pregnancies.

Pope John Paul II. "To the Bishops, Priests and Deacons, Men and Women religious lay Faithful, and all People of Good Will on the Value and Inviolability of Human Life." *Evangelium Vitae*, 1995.

Pope Pius XII. "Address to Midwives on the Nature of Their Profession." *Papal Encyclical*, October 29, 1951.

Progressive Anti-Abortion Uprising. "Stances: Capitalism." Accessed May 3, 2023. https://paaunow.org/stances-capitalism.

Protopapas, Valerie H. "Abortion, Oikonomia and the Hard Cases: The Position of the Church on Abortion," Pemptousia (website),

St. Maxim the Greek Institute, April 20, 2016. https://pemptousia.com/2016/04/the-position-of-the-church-on-abortion-2/.

Reardon, David, and Tessa Longbons. "Effects of Pressure to Abort on Women's Emotional Responses and Mental Health." *Cureus* 15(1), (January 31, 2023): e34456. doi:10.7759/cureus.34456.

Reardon, David, Julie Makimaa, and Amy Sobie, eds. *Victims and Victors: Speaking Out About Their Pregnancies, Abortions, and Children Resulting from Sexual Assault.* Springfield: Acorn Books, 2000, Kindle edition 2022.

Roberts, Alexander, and James Donaldson, eds. *The Ante-Nicene Fathers: Translations of the Writings of the Fathers Down to AD 325.* New York: Charles Scribner's Sons, 1903. Quoted in Mike Aquilina, *The Witness of Early Christian Women: Mothers of the Church*. Huntington: Our Sunday Visitor Publishing, 2014.

Roets, Ellen, Sigrid Dierickx, Luc Deliens, Kenneth Chambaere, Laure Dombrecht, Kristien Roelens and Kim Beernaert. "Healthcare professionals' attitudes towards termination of pregnancy at viable stage." *Acta Obstetricia et Gynecologica Scandinavica* 100(1), (January 2021): 74-83. https://doi.org/10.1111/aogs.13967.

Sabourin, Jeanelle, and Margaret Burnett. "A Review of Therapeutic Abortions and Related Areas of Concern in Canada," *Journal of Obstetrics and Gynecology* 34(6), June 2012: 532–542.

Sartre, Jean-Paul. "Existentialism Is a Humanism." In *Jean-Paul Sartre: Basic Writings*. Translated by Stephen Priest. London: Routledge, 2001.

Schnittman, Suzanne. "Elizabeth Cady Stanton: Feminist, Wife and Mother of Seven," Feminists for Life of America. Accessed May 11, 2023. https://www.feministsforlife.org/elizabeth-cady-stanton-feminist-wife-and-mother-of-seven.

Singer, Peter. FAQ #9. Accessed May 3, 2023. https://petersinger.info/faq.

Singer, Peter. *Rethinking Life and Death.* New York: St. Martin's Press, 1994.

Smith, Westley J. "Infanticide Becomes Justifiable." *First Things*, February 6, 2019. https://www.firstthings.com/web-exclusives/2019/02/infanticide-becomes-justifiable.

Society of Obstetricians and Gynaecologists of Canada. "Unintended Pregnancy." Accessed May 5, 2023. https://www.pregnancyinfo.ca/your-pregnancy/special-consideration/unintended-pregnancy/.

Spellecy, Colleen Kelly, and Eric Anthony. "Yes, Susan B. Anthony Was Pro-Life: She and Elizabeth Cady Stanton railed against abortion in the pages of their paper." *The Wall Street Journal.* June 13, 2022.

Spiro, Ken. *World Perfect: The Jewish Impact on Civilization.* Deerfield Beach: Simcha Press, 2002.

Stager, Lawrence. "Eroticism and Infanticide at Ashkelon," *Biblical Archeology Review*, July 1991.

Stagg, Evelyn, and Frank Stagg. "Jesus and Women." Christian History, *Christianity Today*, 1988.

Stanton, Glenn T. "The History of Christianity and Abortion." Focus on the Family USA, August 19, 2022.

Stark, Rodney. *The Rise of Christianity: How the Obscure, Marginal Jesus Movement Became the Dominant Religious Force in the Western World in a Few Centuries.* New York: HarperOne, 1996.

Supreme Court of the United States. 19-1392 *Dobbs v. Jackson Women's Health Organization.* June 24, 2022, https://www.supremecourt.gov/opinions/21pdf/19-1392_6j37.pdf?ref=sdnewswatch.org.

Teresa, Mother. "Mother Teresa's 1994 Message to the Supreme Court on Abortion." *Public Discourse: The Journal of the Witherspoon Institute.* Posted

September 5, 2016. https://www.thepublicdiscourse.com/2016/09/17771/.

Tertullian. *Apology.* 9.8. AD 197.

Tertullian. *De Anima.* c. AD 203.

The Right to Life Charitable Trust. "94% of Belgian doctors surveyed support 'after-birth abortion' for babies with disabilities." *Right to Life News*, United Kingdom, August 10, 2020. https://righttolife.org.uk/news/94-of-belgian-doctors-surveyed-support-after-birth-abortion-for-babies-with-disabilities.

The Salvation Army International. "Positional Statement: Abortion." High Council of The Salvation Army, November 2010. Accessed July 19, 2023. https://www.salvationarmy.org/ihq/ipsabortion.

Thielicke, Helmut. *The Ethics of Sex.* Chap. B. New York: Harper and Row, 1964.

United States Conference of Catholic Bishops. "Respect for Unborn Human Life: The Church's Constant Teaching." Accessed March 11, 2023. https://www.usccb.org/issues-and-action/human-life-and-dignity/abortion/respect-for-unborn-human-life.

Urquia, Marcelo, Rahim Moineddin, Prabhat Jha, Patricia O'Campo, Kwame McKenzie, Richard

Glazier, David Henry and Joel Ray. "Sex Ratios as Birth after Induced Abortion." *Canadian Medical Association Journal* 188(9), (June 14, 2016): e181-e190.

Verhagen, Eduard, and Pieter J. J. Sauer. "The Groningen Protocol—Euthanasia in Severely Ill Newborns." *The New England Journal of Medicine* 352(10), (March 10, 2005): 959-962.

Waltke, Bruce. "Love, Justice and the Allocation of Limited Medical Resources." In *Questions of Right and Wrong: The Proceedings of the 1993 Clinical Bioethics Conference*, edited by Edwin C. Hui, 75-91. Vancouver: Regent College, 1994.

We Need a Law. "Canadian Opinions on Abortion: Abortion Polls Summarized." June 4, 2020. https://weneedalaw.ca/ 2020/06/ canadian-opinions-on-abortion.

Webster, Alexander. "An Orthodox Word on Abortion." Paper delivered at the Consultation on the Church and Abortion, Princeton, 1992.

Weigel, George. "To Defend the Disposable." *First Things*, December 31, 2014.

Williams, Sarah. "History of Christianity I" course. Vancouver: Regent College audio, 2017.

Wolfensberger, Wolf. *The New Genocide of Handicapped and Afflicted People.* New York: Syracuse University School of Education, 2005.

Wood, David. "Early Church Expansion, Life and Worship." Class lectures at Pacific Life Bible College, Surrey, BC, 2022.

World Vision International. "2018 International Conference on Family Planning." Accessed August 2, 2023. https://www.worldvision.org/our-work/health/icfp2018.

Wright, N.T. "American Christians and the death penalty." *Washington Post.* September 15, 2011. Accessed on Virtueonline, September 14, 2022. https://virtueonline.org/american-christians-and-death-penalty-n-t-wright.

ABOUT THE AUTHOR

Brian Norton holds a Master of Ministry, Bachelor of Political Science, Professional Teacher Certificate, Minor in Environmental Education, and social work in-service accreditation.

For eight years, Brian was a social worker in child protection services and assisting families with children with special needs. For thirty years, Brian served as co-founder and executive director of the Christian Advocacy Society of Greater Vancouver, a charity providing sexual assault recovery, shelter for abused women and children, help for women experiencing unexpected pregnancies, and post-abortion care. Brian is also co-founder and a board member with Pregnancy Care Canada, a national best practice association for affiliated pregnancy centres.

Brian's wife, Judi, is a judicial case manager. When presiding on the bench, Judi is addressed as Your Worship, just like at home. They have three venturesome adult daughters, three sons-in-law who traded up (so say the gals), and seven adorable grandchildren (undisputed).